I AM THEODORE
Lyla
Sophie
lexie
J is for Jacob
my name is Billy
Georgia

Martha
BETH
Jace
penny
I am
Oliver
Rory
M is for Maria

Written for my two beautiful daughters Isobelle and Emelia.

Unite, inspire, be compassionate and kind.

Make a difference and be different...

"Because if we were all the same,
The world would be a boring place
And that would be a shame."

KNOW ME BY MY

WRITTEN BY KIRSTY WEBB
ILLUSTRATED BY LAUREANA AUTY

Hello there, how do you do?
My name is Little Rory,
I'd like to take you on a journey
And tell you about my story.

My story is very different
To others you may have heard,
But that's kind of the point
Because 'different' is my favourite word.

Some people think that ‘different’
Is not what you want to be,
But listen to my story
And soon I think you’ll see.

For you are different to me
And I am different to you,
So know me by my name
And not the different things I do.

R
O
R
y

My name is Little Rory
And there is something I'd like you to know.
I have autism
And sometimes it might show.

I don't really like loud noises
And might not look you in the eye,
But that doesn't mean I'm not listening
I'm just a little shy.

Lots of people have autism
We show it in different ways,
Some of us don't talk too much
And some can talk for days.

Some of us might stutter
Or say things we don't mean,
Sometimes we get over-excited
And sometimes we might scream.

My name is Little Rory
I'm autistic but that's okay,
Don't be scared to talk to me
And please don't run away.

I will be your friend
I'm just different to you,
But don't forget my story
- You are different too.

Hello there, how do you do?
Penny is my name,
I am Little Rory's friend
And we are not the same.

I am not the same as Rory
And I am not the same as you,
But listen to our story
Because you are different too.

I was born with something special
They call it Down syndrome,
I might look a little different
As I have an extra chromosome.

penny

Lots of people have Down syndrome
You might even be able to tell,
We might look very similar
But we are different as well.

Sometimes we might struggle to talk
Or need extra help at school,
We might be shy and hide away
Or may not be shy at all.

Don't be scared to talk to us,
Please don't hide away,
Our differences are wonderful
And we do still love to play.

My name is Little Penny
And my friend is Little Rory,
We are both very different
And this is our 'different' story.

You are different to me
And I am different to you,
So know me by my name
And not the different things I do.

Hello there how do you do
My name is Theodore,
I am Rory and Penny's friend
And I'd like to tell you more.

I am also different
And I'd like to tell you why,
I cannot walk too well
So my wheelchair helps me fly.

I was born with Cerebral Palsy
So my muscles are a little weak,
It can be hard to do things
Like playing hide and seek.

It doesn't mean I can't join in
Some help is all I need,
I may be a little clumsy
But with help I will succeed.

Lots of people have Cerebral Palsy
It affects us in different ways,
You may not understand us
As some words can be hard to say.

Our limbs might be a little wobbly
Or sometimes we might shake,
But maybe if you understand
That's all that it will take.

Go Theodore!

My name is Theodore
My friends are Penny and Rory,
If you listen carefully
You might just understand our story.

You are different to me
And I am different to you,
So know me by my name
And not the different things I do.

Hello there my name is Sophie
And I am different as well,
Maybe not how you'd expect
But I will tell you how.

I cannot hear you because I am deaf
So I listen in a different way,
I will watch you carefully
And see what you have to say.

People talk to me in sign language
By moving around their hands,
This means I need to watch them close
Until I understand.

Lots of people cannot hear
So be patient and be kind,
Because if you try to understand
A new friend we both might find.

Sophie

Maybe you are just like us
Or maybe not at all,
Maybe you are really big
Or maybe you are small.

Maybe you wear glasses
Have one arm or maybe two,
Maybe you can't talk too well
Or do things that we can do.

Being different can be so much fun
Because if we were all the same,
The world would be a boring place
And that would be a shame.

I hope you understand
Our very different story,
Because you are also different
Like Penny, Theo and Rory.

For you are different to me
And I am different to you,
So know us all by name
And not the different things we do.

Why don't you try signing your own name like Sophie using the British Sign Language images below?
– Ask an adult if you need help.

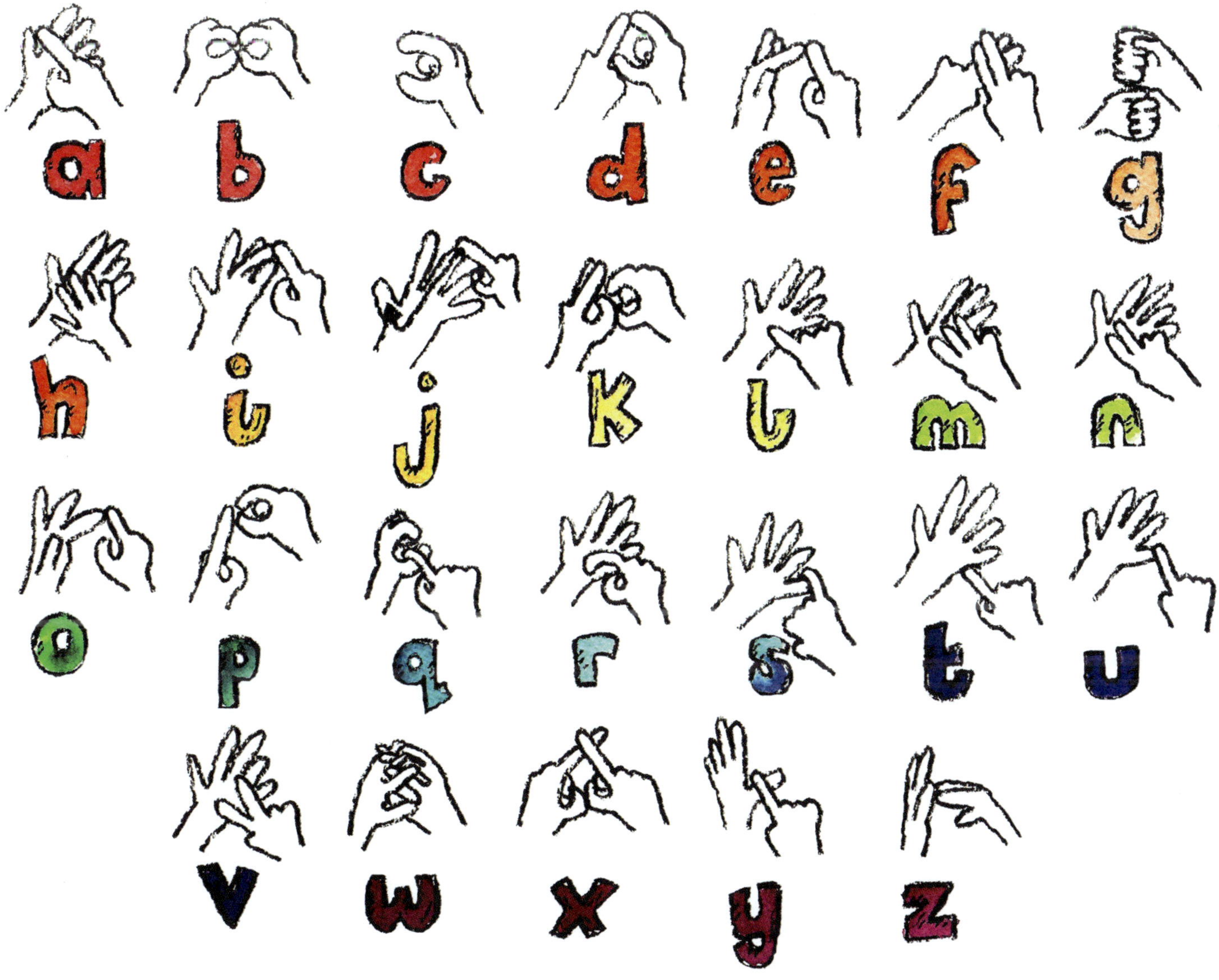

First paperback edition first published in 2019

Cover Design and book design by Rachel Bostwick

Printed in Poland
by Amazon Fulfillment
Poland Sp. z o.o., Wrocław

54091594R00023